50 Healthy Start Recipes for Home

By: Kelly Johnson

Table of Contents

- Avocado Bacon Egg Cups
- Cauliflower Mac and Cheese
- Keto Pizza with Almond Flour Crust
- Zucchini Noodles with Pesto
- Eggplant Lasagna
- Keto Beef Stir-Fry
- Baked Chicken Thighs with Rosemary
- Keto Cheeseburger Salad
- Cauliflower Fried Rice
- Keto Pancakes
- Grilled Salmon with Lemon Butter Sauce
- Keto Meatballs in Marinara Sauce
- Chicken and Broccoli Alfredo
- Keto Chocolate Mousse
- Keto Egg Salad
- Garlic Parmesan Roasted Brussels Sprouts
- Keto Buffalo Chicken Wings
- Coconut Flour Tortillas
- Keto Steak with Garlic Butter
- Keto Chicken Parmesan
- Spaghetti Squash Carbonara
- Keto Zucchini Fritters
- Shrimp Scampi with Zoodles
- Keto Cauliflower Pizza Bites
- Keto Avocado Toast on Cloud Bread
- Keto Bacon-Wrapped Asparagus
- Keto Chocolate Chip Cookies
- Keto Chia Pudding
- Keto Beef and Broccoli
- Chicken and Spinach Stuffed Mushrooms
- Keto Creamy Mushroom Soup
- Keto Meatloaf
- Cabbage Stir-Fry with Pork
- Keto Garlic Butter Shrimp
- Keto Avocado Chicken Salad

- Keto Chicken Soup
- Keto Deviled Eggs
- Keto Turkey Lettuce Wraps
- Keto Cauliflower Mashed Potatoes
- Keto Pumpkin Spice Muffins
- Keto Salmon Cakes
- Keto Coconut Flour Bread
- Keto Broccoli and Cheese Casserole
- Keto Chocolate Fat Bombs
- Keto Beef Tacos with Lettuce Wraps
- Keto Cauliflower Baked Mac and Cheese
- Keto Almond Joy Fat Bombs
- Keto BBQ Chicken
- Keto Spinach and Cheese Stuffed Chicken Breast
- Keto Cabbage Slaw

Avocado Bacon Egg Cups

Ingredients:

- 2 ripe avocados
- 4 eggs
- 4 slices cooked bacon, crumbled
- Salt and pepper to taste
- Fresh herbs (optional)

Instructions:

1. Preheat the oven to 375°F (190°C).
2. Cut the avocados in half and remove the pit. Scoop out a small amount of flesh to create space for the egg.
3. Place the avocado halves in a baking dish.
4. Crack one egg into each avocado half.
5. Sprinkle with crumbled bacon, salt, and pepper.
6. Bake for 15-20 minutes, until the egg whites are set.
7. Garnish with fresh herbs if desired and serve.

Cauliflower Mac and Cheese

Ingredients:

- 1 medium cauliflower head, cut into florets
- 1 cup shredded cheddar cheese
- 1/2 cup cream cheese
- 1/2 cup heavy cream
- 1/2 teaspoon garlic powder
- Salt and pepper to taste

Instructions:

1. Steam or boil the cauliflower florets until tender, about 5-7 minutes.
2. In a saucepan, melt the cream cheese and heavy cream together, stirring to combine.
3. Add the shredded cheddar cheese and garlic powder, stirring until smooth.
4. Add the cooked cauliflower to the sauce and mash lightly to combine.
5. Season with salt and pepper and serve.

Keto Pizza with Almond Flour Crust

Ingredients for Crust:

- 1 1/2 cups almond flour
- 2 tablespoons ground flaxseed
- 1/4 teaspoon baking powder
- 1/4 teaspoon salt
- 1 egg
- 1 tablespoon olive oil

Ingredients for Toppings:

- 1/2 cup sugar-free tomato sauce
- 1 1/2 cups shredded mozzarella cheese
- 1/2 cup pepperoni slices (optional)
- Fresh basil leaves (optional)

Instructions:

1. Preheat the oven to 400°F (200°C).
2. In a bowl, combine almond flour, flaxseed, baking powder, salt, egg, and olive oil. Mix until a dough forms.
3. Roll out the dough between two sheets of parchment paper to desired thickness.
4. Bake the crust for 10-12 minutes, until golden brown.
5. Spread tomato sauce on the baked crust, then top with mozzarella and pepperoni.
6. Bake for another 5-7 minutes until the cheese is melted and bubbly.
7. Garnish with fresh basil and serve.

Zucchini Noodles with Pesto

Ingredients:

- 2 medium zucchinis, spiralized
- 1/2 cup basil pesto (store-bought or homemade)
- 1 tablespoon olive oil
- Salt and pepper to taste
- Parmesan cheese for garnish (optional)

Instructions:

1. Heat olive oil in a pan over medium heat. Add the zucchini noodles and cook for 3-5 minutes, stirring occasionally, until tender.
2. Stir in the pesto and cook for another 2 minutes, until well coated.
3. Season with salt and pepper.
4. Garnish with Parmesan cheese, if desired, and serve.

Eggplant Lasagna

Ingredients:

- 2 medium eggplants, sliced into 1/4-inch thick rounds
- 2 cups ricotta cheese
- 1 egg
- 1/4 cup grated Parmesan cheese
- 2 cups marinara sauce
- 2 cups shredded mozzarella cheese
- Salt and pepper to taste

Instructions:

1. Preheat the oven to 375°F (190°C).
2. Lay the eggplant slices on a baking sheet and bake for 10 minutes until tender.
3. In a bowl, mix ricotta, egg, Parmesan, salt, and pepper.
4. Spread a layer of marinara sauce in a baking dish. Layer eggplant slices, ricotta mixture, and mozzarella. Repeat layers, finishing with mozzarella on top.
5. Bake for 25-30 minutes, until bubbly and golden.
6. Let cool for a few minutes before serving.

Keto Beef Stir-Fry

Ingredients:

- 1 lb beef sirloin, thinly sliced
- 1 tablespoon olive oil
- 1 bell pepper, sliced
- 1 medium zucchini, sliced
- 1 tablespoon soy sauce (or coconut aminos)
- 1 teaspoon garlic powder
- 1/2 teaspoon ground ginger
- Salt and pepper to taste

Instructions:

1. Heat olive oil in a pan over medium-high heat. Add the beef and stir-fry for 3-4 minutes until browned.
2. Add the bell pepper and zucchini and cook for an additional 5-7 minutes until vegetables are tender.
3. Stir in soy sauce, garlic powder, ginger, salt, and pepper.
4. Cook for another 2-3 minutes and serve.

Baked Chicken Thighs with Rosemary

Ingredients:

- 4 bone-in, skin-on chicken thighs
- 2 tablespoons olive oil
- 1 tablespoon fresh rosemary, chopped
- 2 cloves garlic, minced
- Salt and pepper to taste

Instructions:

1. Preheat the oven to 400°F (200°C).
2. Rub the chicken thighs with olive oil, rosemary, garlic, salt, and pepper.
3. Place the thighs on a baking sheet and bake for 35-40 minutes, until the chicken is fully cooked and the skin is crispy.
4. Serve with a side of vegetables or salad.

Keto Cheeseburger Salad

Ingredients:

- 1 lb ground beef
- 4 cups mixed greens
- 1 cup cherry tomatoes, halved
- 1/2 cup shredded cheddar cheese
- 1/4 cup pickles, chopped
- 1/4 cup red onion, thinly sliced
- 1/4 cup mayonnaise
- 2 tablespoons mustard
- Salt and pepper to taste

Instructions:

1. Cook the ground beef in a skillet over medium heat until browned, then drain excess fat.
2. In a large bowl, toss together mixed greens, tomatoes, cheddar cheese, pickles, and red onion.
3. In a small bowl, mix mayonnaise, mustard, salt, and pepper to make the dressing.
4. Top the salad with the cooked beef and drizzle with dressing. Serve immediately.

Cauliflower Fried Rice

Ingredients:

- 1 medium cauliflower head, grated into rice-sized pieces
- 1 tablespoon sesame oil
- 2 eggs, beaten
- 1/2 cup frozen peas and carrots
- 2 green onions, sliced
- 2 tablespoons soy sauce (or coconut aminos)
- Salt and pepper to taste

Instructions:

1. Heat sesame oil in a pan over medium heat. Add the eggs and scramble until cooked.
2. Add the peas and carrots, cauliflower rice, and soy sauce. Stir-fry for 5-7 minutes until cauliflower is tender.
3. Season with salt and pepper and top with green onions. Serve warm.

Keto Pancakes

Ingredients:

- 1 cup almond flour
- 2 large eggs
- 1/4 cup unsweetened almond milk
- 1 teaspoon baking powder
- 1/2 teaspoon vanilla extract
- Pinch of salt

Instructions:

1. In a bowl, whisk together almond flour, eggs, almond milk, baking powder, vanilla extract, and salt.
2. Heat a non-stick pan over medium heat and lightly grease with butter or oil.
3. Pour small portions of batter onto the pan and cook until bubbles form, then flip and cook the other side for another 2-3 minutes.
4. Serve with sugar-free syrup or berries.

Grilled Salmon with Lemon Butter Sauce

Ingredients:

- 4 salmon fillets
- 2 tablespoons olive oil
- 2 tablespoons butter
- 2 cloves garlic, minced
- Juice of 1 lemon
- Salt and pepper to taste

Instructions:

1. Preheat the grill to medium-high heat.
2. Brush salmon fillets with olive oil and season with salt and pepper.
3. Grill salmon for 4-6 minutes per side until cooked through.
4. In a saucepan, melt butter over medium heat, then add garlic and cook for 1 minute.
5. Stir in lemon juice and season with salt and pepper.
6. Drizzle the lemon butter sauce over the grilled salmon and serve.

Keto Meatballs in Marinara Sauce

Ingredients:

- 1 lb ground beef or turkey
- 1/4 cup almond flour
- 1 egg
- 2 cloves garlic, minced
- 1/4 cup grated Parmesan cheese
- 1 tsp Italian seasoning
- Salt and pepper to taste
- 1 1/2 cups sugar-free marinara sauce
- Fresh basil for garnish (optional)

Instructions:

1. Preheat the oven to 375°F (190°C).
2. In a bowl, mix ground meat, almond flour, egg, garlic, Parmesan, Italian seasoning, salt, and pepper.
3. Roll the mixture into small meatballs and place on a baking sheet.
4. Bake for 15-20 minutes or until cooked through.
5. While meatballs bake, heat marinara sauce in a saucepan over low heat.
6. Once the meatballs are done, add them to the marinara sauce and simmer for 5-10 minutes.
7. Serve hot, garnished with fresh basil.

Chicken and Broccoli Alfredo

Ingredients:

- 2 boneless, skinless chicken breasts, cooked and sliced
- 2 cups broccoli florets, steamed
- 1 cup heavy cream
- 1/2 cup grated Parmesan cheese
- 1/4 cup butter
- 2 cloves garlic, minced
- Salt and pepper to taste
- Fresh parsley for garnish (optional)

Instructions:

1. In a saucepan, melt butter over medium heat and sauté garlic until fragrant (about 1-2 minutes).
2. Add heavy cream and bring to a simmer, stirring occasionally.
3. Stir in Parmesan cheese until the sauce thickens.
4. Add cooked chicken and steamed broccoli to the sauce, stirring to coat.
5. Season with salt and pepper to taste.
6. Garnish with fresh parsley and serve.

Keto Chocolate Mousse

Ingredients:

- 1 cup heavy cream
- 3 tbsp unsweetened cocoa powder
- 2 tbsp powdered erythritol (or other sweetener)
- 1/2 tsp vanilla extract
- Pinch of salt

Instructions:

1. In a mixing bowl, beat heavy cream until stiff peaks form.
2. In a separate bowl, whisk together cocoa powder, sweetener, vanilla, and salt.
3. Gently fold the cocoa mixture into the whipped cream until combined.
4. Serve immediately or refrigerate for 30 minutes for a firmer texture.

Keto Egg Salad

Ingredients:

- 6 hard-boiled eggs, chopped
- 1/4 cup mayonnaise
- 1 tsp Dijon mustard
- 1 tbsp fresh chives, chopped
- Salt and pepper to taste

Instructions:

1. In a bowl, mix chopped eggs, mayonnaise, Dijon mustard, and chives.
2. Stir to combine, and season with salt and pepper to taste.
3. Serve as is or in lettuce wraps for a low-carb option.

Garlic Parmesan Roasted Brussels Sprouts

Ingredients:

- 2 cups Brussels sprouts, halved
- 2 tbsp olive oil
- 3 cloves garlic, minced
- 1/4 cup grated Parmesan cheese
- Salt and pepper to taste

Instructions:

1. Preheat the oven to 400°F (200°C).
2. Toss Brussels sprouts with olive oil, garlic, salt, and pepper.
3. Roast for 20-25 minutes, flipping halfway through.
4. Remove from the oven, sprinkle with Parmesan cheese, and serve.

Keto Buffalo Chicken Wings

Ingredients:

- 10-12 chicken wings
- 1/2 cup buffalo sauce
- 2 tbsp butter, melted
- Salt to taste

Instructions:

1. Preheat the oven to 400°F (200°C).
2. Season chicken wings with salt and bake for 25-30 minutes until crispy.
3. In a small bowl, mix melted butter with buffalo sauce.
4. Toss the cooked wings in the buffalo sauce mixture and serve.

Coconut Flour Tortillas

Ingredients:

- 1/4 cup coconut flour
- 2 large eggs
- 2 tbsp melted butter
- 1/4 tsp salt
- 1/4 tsp baking powder
- Water as needed

Instructions:

1. In a bowl, whisk together coconut flour, eggs, melted butter, salt, and baking powder.
2. Slowly add water to form a dough that is pliable.
3. Roll out the dough between two sheets of parchment paper into thin circles.
4. Cook tortillas in a non-stick pan over medium heat for 1-2 minutes per side.
5. Serve warm.

Keto Steak with Garlic Butter

Ingredients:

- 2 ribeye steaks
- 2 tbsp butter
- 2 cloves garlic, minced
- 1 tbsp fresh thyme or rosemary (optional)
- Salt and pepper to taste

Instructions:

1. Season steaks with salt and pepper.
2. Heat a cast-iron skillet over medium-high heat and cook steaks to desired doneness (4-5 minutes per side for medium-rare).
3. While the steaks are cooking, melt butter in a small saucepan with garlic and herbs.
4. Once steaks are done, drizzle with garlic butter and serve.

Keto Chicken Parmesan

Ingredients:

- 2 boneless, skinless chicken breasts
- 1/2 cup almond flour
- 1 egg, beaten
- 1/2 cup grated Parmesan cheese
- 1/2 cup marinara sauce (sugar-free)
- 1/2 cup shredded mozzarella cheese
- Olive oil for frying
- Salt and pepper to taste

Instructions:

1. Preheat the oven to 375°F (190°C).
2. Coat the chicken breasts in almond flour, dip in the egg, then coat with Parmesan cheese.
3. Heat olive oil in a skillet and cook chicken breasts for 3-4 minutes per side until golden.
4. Place chicken breasts in a baking dish, top with marinara sauce and mozzarella.
5. Bake for 15-20 minutes until cheese is melted and bubbly.
6. Serve hot.

Spaghetti Squash Carbonara

Ingredients:

- 1 medium spaghetti squash
- 4 slices bacon, chopped
- 1/2 cup heavy cream
- 2 large eggs
- 1/2 cup Parmesan cheese, grated
- 2 cloves garlic, minced
- Salt and pepper to taste
- Fresh parsley for garnish (optional)

Instructions:

1. Preheat oven to 400°F (200°C). Cut the spaghetti squash in half and remove the seeds.
2. Place squash halves cut-side down on a baking sheet and roast for 30-40 minutes until tender.
3. In a skillet, cook bacon until crispy, then remove and set aside. In the same skillet, sauté garlic in bacon grease for 1 minute.
4. In a bowl, whisk together eggs, heavy cream, Parmesan, salt, and pepper.
5. Once the squash is cooked, scrape the flesh with a fork to create "noodles."
6. Toss the squash noodles in the bacon and garlic mixture. Remove from heat, then add the egg mixture and toss quickly to create a creamy sauce.
7. Garnish with crispy bacon and parsley before serving.

Keto Zucchini Fritters

Ingredients:

- 2 medium zucchinis, grated
- 1/4 cup almond flour
- 1/4 cup grated Parmesan cheese
- 1 egg
- 2 cloves garlic, minced
- Salt and pepper to taste
- Olive oil for frying

Instructions:

1. Place the grated zucchini in a clean kitchen towel and squeeze out excess moisture.
2. In a bowl, combine zucchini, almond flour, Parmesan, egg, garlic, salt, and pepper.
3. Heat olive oil in a skillet over medium heat.
4. Form the zucchini mixture into small fritters and fry for 2-3 minutes per side until golden brown.
5. Remove from heat and serve warm.

Shrimp Scampi with Zoodles

Ingredients:

- 1 lb large shrimp, peeled and deveined
- 4 zucchinis, spiralized into noodles (zoodles)
- 4 cloves garlic, minced
- 2 tbsp olive oil
- 1/4 cup dry white wine (or chicken broth)
- 1/4 cup fresh lemon juice
- 1/4 cup Parmesan cheese
- Salt and pepper to taste
- Fresh parsley for garnish

Instructions:

1. In a large skillet, heat olive oil over medium heat and sauté garlic for 1 minute.
2. Add shrimp to the skillet and cook for 2-3 minutes per side until pink.
3. Remove shrimp from the skillet and set aside. In the same skillet, add white wine and lemon juice, cooking for 2 minutes.
4. Add zoodles and cook for 2-3 minutes until tender.
5. Return shrimp to the skillet and toss to coat with the sauce. Sprinkle with Parmesan and fresh parsley.
6. Serve immediately.

Keto Cauliflower Pizza Bites

Ingredients:

- 1 medium cauliflower, grated
- 1/4 cup Parmesan cheese
- 1/4 cup shredded mozzarella cheese
- 1 egg
- 1 tsp dried oregano
- Salt and pepper to taste
- Tomato sauce for dipping

Instructions:

1. Preheat oven to 400°F (200°C). Line a baking sheet with parchment paper.
2. Microwave grated cauliflower for 5-7 minutes until soft. Let cool slightly, then squeeze out excess moisture.
3. In a bowl, combine cauliflower, Parmesan, mozzarella, egg, oregano, salt, and pepper.
4. Form small pizza bites and place them on the baking sheet.
5. Bake for 15-20 minutes until golden and crispy.
6. Serve with tomato sauce for dipping.

Keto Avocado Toast on Cloud Bread

Ingredients:

- 2 slices cloud bread (store-bought or homemade)
- 1 ripe avocado
- 1 tbsp lemon juice
- Salt and pepper to taste
- Red pepper flakes (optional)

Instructions:

1. Toast the cloud bread slices.
2. Mash the avocado with lemon juice, salt, and pepper.
3. Spread the mashed avocado onto the toasted cloud bread.
4. Sprinkle with red pepper flakes if desired.
5. Serve immediately.

Keto Bacon-Wrapped Asparagus

Ingredients:

- 1 bunch asparagus, trimmed
- 8 slices bacon
- Olive oil for drizzling
- Salt and pepper to taste

Instructions:

1. Preheat oven to 400°F (200°C).
2. Wrap each asparagus spear with a slice of bacon, securing with toothpicks if necessary.
3. Place wrapped asparagus on a baking sheet and drizzle with olive oil.
4. Roast for 20-25 minutes, until bacon is crispy and asparagus is tender.
5. Serve hot.

Keto Chocolate Chip Cookies

Ingredients:

- 1 1/4 cups almond flour
- 1/4 cup unsweetened cocoa powder
- 1/4 cup coconut flour
- 1/2 tsp baking soda
- 1/4 cup butter, softened
- 1/4 cup erythritol or other sweetener
- 1 egg
- 1 tsp vanilla extract
- 1/2 cup sugar-free chocolate chips

Instructions:

1. Preheat oven to 350°F (175°C). Line a baking sheet with parchment paper.
2. In a bowl, combine almond flour, cocoa powder, coconut flour, and baking soda.
3. In a separate bowl, beat butter and sweetener together until creamy. Add egg and vanilla extract and mix.
4. Gradually combine the dry ingredients with the wet ingredients. Stir in chocolate chips.
5. Scoop dough onto the baking sheet and bake for 10-12 minutes.
6. Let cool before serving.

Keto Chia Pudding

Ingredients:

- 1/4 cup chia seeds
- 1 cup unsweetened almond milk
- 1 tbsp erythritol or sweetener of choice
- 1 tsp vanilla extract

Instructions:

1. In a jar or bowl, combine chia seeds, almond milk, sweetener, and vanilla.
2. Stir well and refrigerate for at least 4 hours or overnight.
3. Stir before serving. Top with berries or nuts if desired.

Keto Beef and Broccoli

Ingredients:

- 1 lb beef (flank steak or sirloin), sliced thinly
- 2 cups broccoli florets
- 2 tbsp soy sauce (or tamari for gluten-free)
- 2 tbsp coconut aminos
- 1 tbsp sesame oil
- 2 cloves garlic, minced
- 1 tbsp ginger, minced
- Salt and pepper to taste
- Sesame seeds for garnish

Instructions:

1. Heat sesame oil in a large skillet over medium heat. Add garlic and ginger and sauté for 1-2 minutes.
2. Add the sliced beef and cook for 3-4 minutes until browned.
3. Add broccoli florets, soy sauce, and coconut aminos, stirring to combine. Cook for 5-7 minutes until broccoli is tender.
4. Season with salt and pepper to taste.
5. Garnish with sesame seeds and serve hot.

Chicken and Spinach Stuffed Mushrooms

Ingredients:

- 12 large mushroom caps, stems removed
- 1 lb cooked chicken breast, shredded
- 1 cup spinach, chopped
- 1/2 cup cream cheese, softened
- 1/4 cup Parmesan cheese, grated
- 1/4 cup mozzarella cheese, shredded
- 1 clove garlic, minced
- Salt and pepper to taste
- Olive oil for drizzling

Instructions:

1. Preheat oven to 375°F (190°C). Place mushroom caps on a baking sheet.
2. In a skillet, sauté garlic in olive oil for 1-2 minutes. Add spinach and cook until wilted.
3. In a bowl, mix shredded chicken, spinach, cream cheese, Parmesan, mozzarella, salt, and pepper.
4. Stuff the mushroom caps with the chicken mixture.
5. Drizzle with olive oil and bake for 20 minutes or until golden and bubbly.
6. Serve hot.

Keto Creamy Mushroom Soup

Ingredients:

- 2 tbsp butter
- 1 lb mushrooms, sliced
- 1 small onion, chopped
- 2 cloves garlic, minced
- 4 cups chicken broth
- 1 cup heavy cream
- Salt and pepper to taste
- Fresh parsley for garnish

Instructions:

1. In a large pot, melt butter over medium heat. Add onions and garlic, sauté until softened.
2. Add sliced mushrooms and cook for 5-7 minutes until tender.
3. Pour in chicken broth and bring to a simmer for 10 minutes.
4. Add heavy cream, salt, and pepper, and simmer for an additional 5 minutes.
5. Use an immersion blender to blend the soup until smooth, or leave some mushrooms chunky for texture.
6. Garnish with fresh parsley and serve.

Keto Meatloaf

Ingredients:

- 1 lb ground beef
- 1/2 cup almond flour
- 1/4 cup grated Parmesan cheese
- 1 egg
- 1/4 cup onion, finely chopped
- 2 cloves garlic, minced
- 1/4 cup sugar-free ketchup
- 1 tbsp Worcestershire sauce
- Salt and pepper to taste

Instructions:

1. Preheat oven to 350°F (175°C). Grease a loaf pan.
2. In a bowl, combine all ingredients, mixing well.
3. Transfer the meat mixture into the loaf pan, shaping it into a loaf.
4. Bake for 40-45 minutes, or until fully cooked.
5. Let rest for 10 minutes before slicing. Serve with your favorite low-carb side.

Cabbage Stir-Fry with Pork

Ingredients:

- 1 lb ground pork
- 4 cups cabbage, shredded
- 1 onion, chopped
- 2 cloves garlic, minced
- 1 tbsp soy sauce (or coconut aminos for a paleo option)
- 1 tbsp sesame oil
- Salt and pepper to taste
- Green onions for garnish

Instructions:

1. In a large skillet or wok, heat sesame oil over medium heat.
2. Add ground pork, cooking until browned.
3. Add onion and garlic, sauté for 2-3 minutes until softened.
4. Stir in shredded cabbage, soy sauce, salt, and pepper. Cook for 5-7 minutes until cabbage is tender.
5. Garnish with green onions and serve.

Keto Garlic Butter Shrimp

Ingredients:

- 1 lb large shrimp, peeled and deveined
- 4 tbsp butter
- 4 cloves garlic, minced
- 1 tbsp lemon juice
- 1/4 tsp red pepper flakes (optional)
- Salt and pepper to taste
- Fresh parsley for garnish

Instructions:

1. In a large skillet, melt butter over medium heat.
2. Add garlic and sauté for 1-2 minutes until fragrant.
3. Add shrimp to the skillet and cook for 2-3 minutes per side, until pink and cooked through.
4. Stir in lemon juice, red pepper flakes (if using), salt, and pepper.
5. Garnish with fresh parsley and serve.

Keto Avocado Chicken Salad

Ingredients:

- 2 cups cooked chicken, shredded
- 1 ripe avocado, mashed
- 1/4 cup mayonnaise
- 1 tbsp lemon juice
- 1/4 cup celery, chopped
- Salt and pepper to taste

Instructions:

1. In a bowl, combine chicken, mashed avocado, mayonnaise, lemon juice, and celery.
2. Mix well, then season with salt and pepper.
3. Serve as a salad or in lettuce wraps.

Keto Chicken Soup

Ingredients:

- 2 tbsp olive oil
- 1 lb chicken breast, cooked and shredded
- 4 cups chicken broth
- 2 celery stalks, chopped
- 1 carrot, chopped
- 1 onion, chopped
- 2 cloves garlic, minced
- 1 tsp dried thyme
- Salt and pepper to taste

Instructions:

1. In a large pot, heat olive oil over medium heat.
2. Add onion, garlic, celery, and carrot. Sauté for 5 minutes until softened.
3. Add chicken broth, chicken, thyme, salt, and pepper. Bring to a boil, then reduce heat and simmer for 20 minutes.
4. Serve hot.

Keto Deviled Eggs

Ingredients:

- 6 large eggs, hard-boiled and peeled
- 1/4 cup mayonnaise
- 1 tsp Dijon mustard
- 1 tbsp vinegar
- Salt and pepper to taste
- Paprika for garnish

Instructions:

1. Cut the hard-boiled eggs in half and remove the yolks.
2. Mash the yolks with mayonnaise, Dijon mustard, vinegar, salt, and pepper.
3. Spoon the yolk mixture back into the egg whites.
4. Garnish with paprika and serve.

Keto Turkey Lettuce Wraps

Ingredients:

- 1 lb ground turkey
- 1 tbsp olive oil
- 1 onion, chopped
- 2 cloves garlic, minced
- 2 tbsp soy sauce (or coconut aminos)
- 1/4 tsp ground ginger
- Salt and pepper to taste
- Romaine lettuce leaves for wrapping

Instructions:

1. In a skillet, heat olive oil over medium heat. Add onion and garlic, sautéing for 3-4 minutes.
2. Add ground turkey, cooking until browned and fully cooked.
3. Stir in soy sauce, ginger, salt, and pepper. Cook for another 2 minutes.
4. Serve the turkey mixture in romaine lettuce leaves as wraps.

Keto Cauliflower Mashed Potatoes

Ingredients:

- 1 medium cauliflower, chopped into florets
- 1/4 cup heavy cream
- 4 tbsp butter
- Salt and pepper to taste
- Garlic powder (optional)

Instructions:

1. Boil the cauliflower in salted water for 8-10 minutes until tender.
2. Drain and mash the cauliflower with butter, heavy cream, salt, and pepper.
3. For extra flavor, add a pinch of garlic powder.
4. Serve hot as a low-carb mashed potato substitute.

Keto Pumpkin Spice Muffins

Ingredients:

- 1 1/2 cups almond flour
- 1/2 cup pumpkin puree
- 1/4 cup erythritol (or preferred sweetener)
- 1/4 cup butter, melted
- 3 large eggs
- 1 tsp baking powder
- 1/2 tsp cinnamon
- 1/4 tsp nutmeg
- 1/4 tsp ginger
- 1/4 tsp salt
- 1 tsp vanilla extract

Instructions:

1. Preheat oven to 350°F (175°C) and line a muffin tin with paper liners.
2. In a large bowl, mix almond flour, erythritol, baking powder, cinnamon, nutmeg, ginger, and salt.
3. Add the pumpkin puree, melted butter, eggs, and vanilla extract. Stir until well combined.
4. Spoon the batter into the muffin cups, filling each about 2/3 full.
5. Bake for 18-20 minutes or until a toothpick comes out clean. Let cool before serving.

Keto Salmon Cakes

Ingredients:

- 2 cans (5 oz each) wild-caught salmon, drained and flaked
- 2 eggs
- 1/4 cup almond flour
- 1/4 cup chopped green onions
- 2 tbsp mayonnaise
- 1 tsp Dijon mustard
- 1/2 tsp garlic powder
- Salt and pepper to taste
- Olive oil for frying

Instructions:

1. In a bowl, combine salmon, eggs, almond flour, green onions, mayonnaise, mustard, garlic powder, salt, and pepper.
2. Mix until well combined and form into patties.
3. Heat olive oil in a skillet over medium heat. Fry the patties for 3-4 minutes per side until golden and crispy.
4. Serve hot with a side salad or dipping sauce.

Keto Coconut Flour Bread

Ingredients:

- 1/4 cup coconut flour
- 1/4 cup almond flour
- 1/2 tsp baking powder
- 1/4 tsp salt
- 3 large eggs
- 1/4 cup unsweetened almond milk
- 2 tbsp melted butter
- 1 tbsp sweetener (optional)
- 1 tsp vanilla extract

Instructions:

1. Preheat oven to 350°F (175°C) and grease a loaf pan.
2. In a bowl, mix coconut flour, almond flour, baking powder, and salt.
3. In another bowl, whisk eggs, almond milk, melted butter, sweetener (if using), and vanilla extract.
4. Combine the wet and dry ingredients and pour the batter into the prepared loaf pan.
5. Bake for 25-30 minutes or until a toothpick inserted comes out clean. Let cool before slicing.

Keto Broccoli and Cheese Casserole

Ingredients:

- 4 cups broccoli florets, steamed
- 1 1/2 cups shredded cheddar cheese
- 1/2 cup heavy cream
- 2 large eggs
- 1/4 cup onion, chopped
- 1/2 tsp garlic powder
- Salt and pepper to taste
- 1/4 cup grated Parmesan cheese

Instructions:

1. Preheat oven to 350°F (175°C) and grease a casserole dish.
2. In a bowl, whisk eggs, heavy cream, garlic powder, salt, and pepper.
3. Add steamed broccoli, cheddar cheese, and chopped onion to the mixture, stirring until well combined.
4. Pour the mixture into the casserole dish and sprinkle with Parmesan cheese.
5. Bake for 25-30 minutes until golden and bubbly. Let cool slightly before serving.

Keto Chocolate Fat Bombs

Ingredients:

- 1/2 cup coconut oil
- 1/4 cup unsweetened cocoa powder
- 1/4 cup almond butter
- 2 tbsp erythritol (or preferred sweetener)
- 1/2 tsp vanilla extract
- Pinch of salt

Instructions:

1. In a small saucepan, melt coconut oil and almond butter over low heat.
2. Stir in cocoa powder, erythritol, vanilla extract, and salt.
3. Pour the mixture into silicone molds or mini muffin tin.
4. Freeze for 30 minutes or until solid. Store in the freezer.

Keto Beef Tacos with Lettuce Wraps

Ingredients:

- 1 lb ground beef
- 1 tbsp olive oil
- 1/4 cup onion, chopped
- 1 packet taco seasoning (or homemade seasoning)
- 1/2 cup beef broth
- Salt and pepper to taste
- Romaine lettuce leaves for wrapping
- Toppings: cheese, sour cream, salsa, avocado

Instructions:

1. Heat olive oil in a skillet over medium heat. Add onion and sauté until softened.
2. Add ground beef and cook until browned, breaking it up as it cooks.
3. Stir in taco seasoning, beef broth, salt, and pepper. Simmer for 5 minutes.
4. Serve the beef mixture in romaine lettuce leaves with desired toppings.

Keto Cauliflower Baked Mac and Cheese

Ingredients:

- 1 large cauliflower head, cut into florets
- 2 cups shredded cheddar cheese
- 1/2 cup heavy cream
- 2 tbsp butter
- 1 tsp garlic powder
- Salt and pepper to taste
- 1/4 cup grated Parmesan cheese

Instructions:

1. Preheat oven to 350°F (175°C) and grease a baking dish.
2. Steam cauliflower florets until tender, about 8-10 minutes.
3. In a saucepan, melt butter over medium heat and add heavy cream, garlic powder, salt, and pepper. Stir in cheddar cheese until melted and smooth.
4. Mix the steamed cauliflower with the cheese sauce and transfer to the baking dish.
5. Sprinkle with Parmesan cheese and bake for 15-20 minutes until bubbly and golden.

Keto Almond Joy Fat Bombs

Ingredients:

- 1/2 cup unsweetened shredded coconut
- 1/4 cup almond butter
- 1/4 cup coconut oil
- 1/4 cup erythritol (or preferred sweetener)
- 1/4 cup almonds, whole or chopped
- 2 tbsp cocoa powder
- 1/2 tsp vanilla extract

Instructions:

1. In a bowl, mix together shredded coconut, almond butter, coconut oil, erythritol, and cocoa powder.
2. Pour the mixture into mini muffin tins or silicone molds.
3. Place an almond in the center of each fat bomb.
4. Freeze for 30 minutes or until solid. Store in the freezer.

Keto BBQ Chicken

Ingredients:

- 4 chicken breasts
- 1/2 cup sugar-free BBQ sauce
- 1 tbsp olive oil
- Salt and pepper to taste
- Fresh parsley for garnish

Instructions:

1. Preheat oven to 375°F (190°C).
2. Rub chicken breasts with olive oil, salt, and pepper.
3. Bake chicken for 20-25 minutes or until cooked through.
4. Brush with BBQ sauce and bake for an additional 5 minutes.
5. Garnish with fresh parsley and serve.

Keto Spinach and Cheese Stuffed Chicken Breast

Ingredients:

- 4 boneless, skinless chicken breasts
- 2 cups fresh spinach, chopped
- 1 cup mozzarella cheese, shredded
- 1/4 cup cream cheese, softened
- 1 clove garlic, minced
- Salt and pepper to taste

Instructions:

1. Preheat oven to 375°F (190°C).
2. In a bowl, mix spinach, mozzarella, cream cheese, garlic, salt, and pepper.
3. Cut a pocket in each chicken breast and stuff with the spinach mixture.
4. Secure with toothpicks and bake for 25-30 minutes or until chicken is fully cooked.
5. Serve hot.

Keto Cabbage Slaw

Ingredients:

- 3 cups shredded cabbage
- 1/2 cup mayonnaise
- 1 tbsp apple cider vinegar
- 1 tbsp Dijon mustard
- 1/2 tsp garlic powder
- Salt and pepper to taste

Instructions:

1. In a large bowl, mix cabbage with mayonnaise, vinegar, Dijon mustard, garlic powder, salt, and pepper.
2. Stir until well combined.
3. Refrigerate for at least 30 minutes before serving.

www.ingramcontent.com/pod-product-compliance
Lightning Source LLC
LaVergne TN
LVHW081338060526
838201LV00055B/2726